Holidays and Festivals

A World of Festivals

Rebecca Rissman

www.raintreepublishers.co.uk
Visit our website to find out more information about Raintree books.

To order:
☎ Phone 0845 6044371
📄 Fax +44 (0) 1865 312263
💻 Email myorders@raintreepublishers.co.uk

Customers from outside the UK please telephone +44 1865 312262

Raintree is an imprint of Capstone Global Library Limited, a company incorporated in England and Wales having its registered office at 7 Pilgrim Street, London, EC4V 6LB – Registered company number: 6695582

Text © Capstone Global Library Limited 2012
First published in hardback in 2012
First published in paperback in 2013
The moral rights of the proprietor have been asserted.

Edited by Daniel Nunn, Rebecca Rissman, and Harriet Milles
Designed by Joanna Hinton-Malivoire
Picture research by Elizabeth Alexander
Originated by Capstone Global Library Ltd.
Production by Victoria Fitzgerald
Printed and bound in China by Leo Paper Products Ltd

ISBN 978 1 406 22900 4 (hardback)
15 14 13 12 11
10 9 8 7 6 5 4 3 2 1

ISBN 978 1 406 22963 9 (paperback)
16 15 14 13 12
10 9 8 7 6 5 4 3 2 1

British Library Cataloguing in Publication Data
Rissman, Rebecca.
   A world of festivals. – (Acorn plus)
   1. Festivals–Pictorial works–Juvenile literature.
   I. Title II. Series
   394.2'6-dc22
A full catalogue record for this book is available from the British Library.

Acknowledgements
We would like to thank the following for permission to reproduce photographs: Alamy **p.11 left** (© Blend Images); Corbis **pp. 8** (© JLP/Jose L. Pelaez), 16 (© T. Mughal/epa); Getty Images **pp. 6** (Leland Bobbe/Stone), 10 (AFP), **17 left** (Jaafar Ashtiyeh/AFP), **17 right** (Asif Hassan/AFP), 18 (Yellow Dog Productions), **19 right** (altrendo images); iStockphoto **p. 21** (© Matt Olsen); Photolibrary **pp. 5 left** (Vidler Vidler), 7 (John Coutts/Britain on View), 12 (Hemant Mehta/India Picture), **15 left** (James and James Photography/Brand X Pictures); Shutterstock **pp. 4** (© michael rubin), **5 right** (© Racheal Grazias), 9 (© Jose Gil), **11 right** (© Hannes Eichinger), **13 left** (© Mahantesh C Morabad), **13 right** (© gmwnz), **14, 15 right** (© Golden Pixels LLC), **20 left & right** (© Monkey Business Images), **19 left** (© haak78), 22 (© Christophe Testi).

Front cover photograph of people watching a fireworks display reproduced with permission of Corbis (© Firefly Productions). Back cover photograph of Chinese children performing reproduced with permission of Shutterstock (© Christophe Testi).

Every effort has been made to contact copyright holders of any material reproduced in this book. Any omissions will be rectified in subsequent printings if notice is given to the publisher.

Contents

Holidays and festivals 4

New Year's Day 8

Easter 10

Divali 12

Hanukkah 14

Ramadan and Id-ul-Fitr 16

Christmas 18

Halloween 20

Bonfire Night 21

How do you celebrate? 22

Words to know 23

Index 24

Notes for parents and teachers 24

Some words appear in bold, **like this**. You can find out what they mean in "Words to know" on page 23.

Holidays and festivals

People celebrate holidays and festivals all around the world. Holidays and festivals are special days. People spend time together and have fun.

Different people celebrate different holidays and festivals. But all holidays and festivals are special.

Some holidays and festivals are part of a **religion** or belief. People who share the same religion gather together to take part in these celebrations.

Some holidays and festivals celebrate a special person who did something good. Other holidays celebrate a country.

New Year's Day

People around the world celebrate the New Year in different ways. The New Year is the start of a new **calendar**. Some people celebrate the New Year on the 1st of January.

Some people celebrate the New Year on different days. Chinese people celebrate New Year on a different day each year. To celebrate the Chinese New Year, people watch **parades** and give gifts.

Easter

Christian people celebrate Easter all around the world.
Many Christian people go to church on Easter Day.
Easter happens in March or April each year.

Easter egg

People celebrate Easter in different ways. On Easter morning, some people hunt for Easter eggs. Some people bake special cakes. Some people eat special food.

Divali

Hindu and Sikh people celebrate Divali all around the world. Divali is called the Festival of Lights. People light special **lanterns** to celebrate Divali.

People celebrate Divali in different ways. Some people draw pictures on their doorsteps. Some people give gifts. Some people dance together and play music.

Hanukkah

menorah

Jewish people celebrate Hanukkah all around the world. Hanukkah lasts for eight nights. People light special candles in a **menorah** to celebrate Hanukkah.

dreidel

People celebrate Hanukkah in different ways. Some people give gifts each day. Some people say prayers each night. Some people eat special foods. Some people play games with **dreidels**.

Ramadan and Id-Ul-Fitr

Muslim people celebrate the month of Ramadan all around the world. During Ramadan, Muslims **fast** from sunrise to sunset. In the evening, families gather to break, or end, the fast together.

At the end of Ramadan, Muslim people celebrate Id-Ul-Fitr. People eat special meals together. Many people give food to the poor.

Christmas

The festival of Christmas celebrates the birth of Jesus Christ. Christmas Day is on the 25th of December. Christian people celebrate Christmas all around the world. Some people have a special tree and a **crib**.

Some people give gifts at Christmas. Some people go to church at Christmas. Some people sing special Christmas songs called **carols**. Some people share a special Christmas dinner.

Halloween

pumpkin

People celebrate Halloween all around the world. Halloween is on the 31st of October. Some people wear fancy dress. Some people carve pumpkins. Some people eat special treats.

Bonfire Night

fireworks

Some people celebrate Bonfire Night on the 5th of November. On Bonfire Night some people light bonfires and watch **fireworks**.

How do you celebrate?

Which is your favourite holiday? How do you like to celebrate it?

Words to know

calendar system used to measure the days and months in a year

carols special songs that people sing at Christmas to celebrate the birth of Jesus Christ

crib model of the stable where the baby Jesus was born

dreidel small spinning top that is used in a special game for Hanukkah

fast time when people do not eat. Many people fast for short times as part of their religion.

fireworks special objects that explode for entertainment. During a fireworks show, many fireworks are set off high in the sky.

lantern special container for a light or candle

menorah candleholder that holds nine candles. Menorahs are used during the Jewish holiday Hanukkah.

parade when people walk together down a street to celebrate an event. Often they wear special clothes.

religion system of beliefs or ideas that people live by

Index

Christian 10, 18

gifts 9, 13, 15, 19

Hindu 12

holidays 4-7, 22

Jewish 14

Muslim 16, 17

religion 6

Sikh 12

Notes for parents and teachers

Before reading

Show the children the front cover of the book. Guide children in a discussion about what they think the book will be about. Can they think of a time they have been to a festival or holiday celebration? Then discuss how people all around the world celebrate holidays and festivals in different ways.

After reading

- Ask the children to think about their favourite holiday or festival. Then ask them to write about their memory explaining why it is their favourite holiday or festival. Encourage them to draw a descriptive picture to go with their writing.